ESCAPING TO AMERICA

A TRUE STORY

ROSALYN SCHANZER

HarperCollinsPublishers

*To the memory of my family
and to everyone who has traveled
from another country to begin
a new life on these shores.*

Escaping to America
Copyright © 2000 by Rosalyn Schanzer

Printed in Singapore at Tien Wah Press.
All rights reserved.

www.harperchildrens.com

Library of Congress Cataloging-in-Publication Data
Schanzer, Rosalyn.
Escaping to America: a true story / Rosalyn Schanzer.
p. cm.
Summary: Tells how the author's family left difficult conditions in Poland to make a
better life for themselves in America early in the twentieth century.
ISBN 0-688-16989-9 (trade) — ISBN 0-688-16990-2 (library)
1. Goodstein family—Juvenile literature.
2. Jews—Poland—Sochocin—Biography—Juvenile literature.
3. Jews, Polish—United States—Biography—Juvenile literature.
4. Sochocin (Poland)—Biography—Juvenile literature.
[1. Goodstein family. 2. Jews—Poland. 3. Poland—Emigration and immigration.]
I. Title. DS135.P63 A163 2000 943.84—dc21 99-53413

1 2 3 4 5 6 7 8 9 10
❖
First Edition

SOCHOCIN, POLAND

1918-1921

MY FAMILY JOURNEYED TO AMERICA LONG BEFORE I WAS BORN.

THEY CAME FROM A TINY TOWN IN POLAND CALLED SOCHOCIN,

AND THEREIN LIES A TALE.

I would like you to meet my grandfather, Abba Goodstein.
Abba's acting and singing were famous. He was full of fun and
loved to stand on his hands and ride on horses upside down.
He could also do wild Russian dances, jumping high into the
air and touching his toes with his fingertips. His strength was
legendary, and he was so smart that he could add up long
columns of big numbers in his head in split seconds.

Abba was married to Pearl, my grandmother. Pearl could play
the mandolin and had a warm smile for everyone. She liked to
draw or sew lacy butterflies and colorful birds with swirling

plumes, and she even designed fancy buttons to be made from seashells in the family's small button factory.

Abba and Pearl also owned a restaurant that was fragrant with the smells of mushroom, herb, and barley soup, slippery homemade noodles, and freshly baked bread. Sometimes plays were performed in the restaurant very late at night.

My grandparents had three children, whose names were Ida, Sammy, and Ruthie. When the family decided to leave their home forever, Ida was four, Sammy was three, and Ruthie was less than one year old. Sammy grew up to be my father.

A fern-filled forest grew all around
the tiny town of Sochocin, and a
river as clear as glass tumbled swiftly
through it. White storks with long
pink legs stood watch from the
chimney tops as geese, goats, and
towering tangles of wildflowers
danced beside winding dirt roads.
In the forest, Ida and Sammy picked
wild berries for breakfast and wild
mushrooms for soup.

But little Sochocin was no paradise. Several different armies were chasing one another across the countryside and fighting a terrible war. Soldiers often stormed into towns without warning and carried off all the food and booty they could find.

One day Abba was standing outside his restaurant when he was surrounded by Cossack soldiers pointing rifles at his chest. Abba smiled fearlessly, and in his most magnificent voice, he started singing a Cossack marching song. The soldiers lowered their rifles and began to laugh and sing and slap Abba on the back. Finally, still singing, they got on their horses and rode away.

Another time three soldiers on horseback attacked the family as they rode in their cart with Pearl's father. They threatened to cut off his long red beard, which his religion forbade him to cut, and one soldier started swinging a bayonet at Abba's neck. Abba knocked the soldier out cold, and the other two rascals fled in fear.

The Goodstein family was Jewish, and many peasants did not like the Jewish religion. Mobs in Sochocin beat up elderly Jews and smashed their shops. Troublemakers accused Jews of being spies, first for one side and then the other. One hot summer afternoon, an honest rabbi wiping his forehead by an open window innocently waved his damp handkerchief out to dry and was shot as a spy trying to send signals to the enemy.

Jews and non-Jews alike dug deep trenches in the rich black soil of their potato fields to hide from flying bullets. And long after midnight, any army in need of new soldiers might burst into the homes of sleeping peasants and take all men of fighting age far away from their families, never to be seen again.

There had been so much shooting that to be safe, the family took shelter in a nearby town. When the fighting died down, they returned to find that soldiers had robbed their house and smashed their restaurant.

Pearl heard that a non-Jewish friend of hers since childhood had led the soldiers to their house and given their belongings away.

"Why did you give away all our things?" she asked.

"You don't need them anymore," the woman replied. "You Jews are all going to be killed anyway."

Life seemed bound to get much worse in Poland. Although nobody was permitted to leave the war zone, Pearl and Abba agreed to find a way out.

The family believed that their best hope for a new life lay in America. But no more Polish people were allowed to enter the country. Abba's older sister, Yitta, had moved to America fourteen years earlier and now lived in Knoxville, Tennessee, with her handsome husband and their four children. Abba wrote a long letter asking if she could help.

Yitta wrote back that she would do her best. First, she traveled all the way to Washington, D.C., to visit her congressman. She convinced him that she would find jobs for her family so that they would be permitted to enter the country. Then she gathered the huge stack of official papers they would need, bought them tickets for passage aboard the Dutch ship *Kroonland,* and sent everything to Poland with a Knoxville woman who took documents to Jewish people moving to America.

By August 1921, everything was ready. Each of the travelers packed one everyday outfit, one dressy outfit, and a pair of galoshes into some wicker suitcases and bundles made of blankets tied with ropes. Only a few small treasures were added: some photographs, a puffy blue comforter filled with goose down, a few handwoven tablecloths and empty pillow covers with fancy tassels, and Pearl's shiny red wedding dress.

Pearl's mother pleaded with her to bring the family's silver Sabbath candlesticks and wine cup, but Pearl could not bear to take these special things away from the family members who decided to stay in Sochocin. Abba and Pearl also knew that soldiers and robbers were likely to take from them anything of value, so everything else they owned and all their money had to be left behind.

The day they left, the travelers and their brothers, sisters, and parents staying behind hung a big fancy blanket and three paintings on the side of a barn. Then they posed for a photograph showing the whole family together for the last time. Everyone was crying.

A clever trick was planned to get out of the war zone without being caught. First everyone hid their luggage beneath a false bottom in a hay wagon. Then Abba took cover underneath a big pile of hay with farm tools sticking out of it, so that he wouldn't be captured by soldiers and drafted into some army—or worse.

Dressed as farmers going to the fields, Pearl and the three children sat in front of the wagon with a driver disguised as a very old man. A pet cow walked beside the wagon to supply milk for the children.

All went well until a cloud of dust arose in the distance. Abba sprinted into the woods, where he could scout ahead without being seen. Many soldiers soon surrounded the wagon and stabbed their sharp bayonets deep into the hay to see if anyone was hiding. They made Pearl trade one of her wagon wheels for a broken one from their supply wagon. Then as the children cried, a soldier took the pet cow to the edge of the road and shot it for food.

The wagon limped slowly toward the town of Plinsk. If they could arrive on time, a train would take the family all the rest of the way to the ship in Danzig. At the last possible moment they arrived at the train station, and wonder of wonders, there was the Knoxville woman bringing all the papers and tickets from America! She even gave a bag of flat rolls shaped like ducks to the children.

To little Sammy's delight, everyone boarded a train with a huge noisy steam engine. Sammy had always loved to pretend

that he was driving a train, but he had never seen one in real life. He saw the scenery flash by out of open glass windows and watched the billowing smoke from the smokestack make the passengers sooty.

At last the family reached the ship bound for America. A flood of other passengers poured inside, wearing colorful clothes from many different countries and speaking in many different languages. The vast blue ocean seemed to sparkle with promise before them.

First-class passengers stayed in fine cabins up on the deck, but the Goodstein family and many others traveling in steerage were packed like sardines down below, where it was dark, smelly, and full of bugs. Passengers stacked up luggage to make their own little areas, using trunks or suitcases as tables. Bunk beds lined the walls, washing water came in small buckets, and bad soup was shared from big pots. There was no such thing as privacy.

Ida joined a throng of children gleefully playing hide-and-seek inside curtained-off bunks, behind stacks of suitcases, and around the ship's big pipes and steps. Then she got the measles.

It soon seemed that everyone was catching the measles. Two sailors closed the exit from steerage atop a big iron stairway so that no one could leave and spread the disease. The filthy hold got terribly hot. It was hard even to breathe. Ida was burning up with fever. If she couldn't reach the fresh cool air on deck, Pearl and Abba were afraid that she would die.

Abba carried Ida up the stairs and explained to the two
guards how much she needed air.

The guards did not care. They roughly tried to push them
both back down the stairs.

Abba had always been a peacemaker, but for the second time
in his life, he was forced to use his fists to save his family. He
knocked each guard down with a single blow. Then he brought
Ida out on deck and held her gently until cooling winds broke
her fever.

Ida soon began to feel better, and before very long she was healthy once again. In spite of the dirty conditions inside the ship, Pearl took special care to keep her children clean during the rest of the voyage.

Just when it seemed that the *Kroonland* would sail the sea forever, an announcement was made. After four long weeks at sea, the voyage to America was almost over. Big excitement! Everyone was allowed on deck, even the passengers who had been crowded into steerage.

Someone passed out small American flags to the children. People could hardly wait to see the Statue of Liberty, and all of a sudden there it was, looking bigger than anyone had imagined. The passengers were laughing and crying, and it seemed as if a million languages were being spoken all at once.

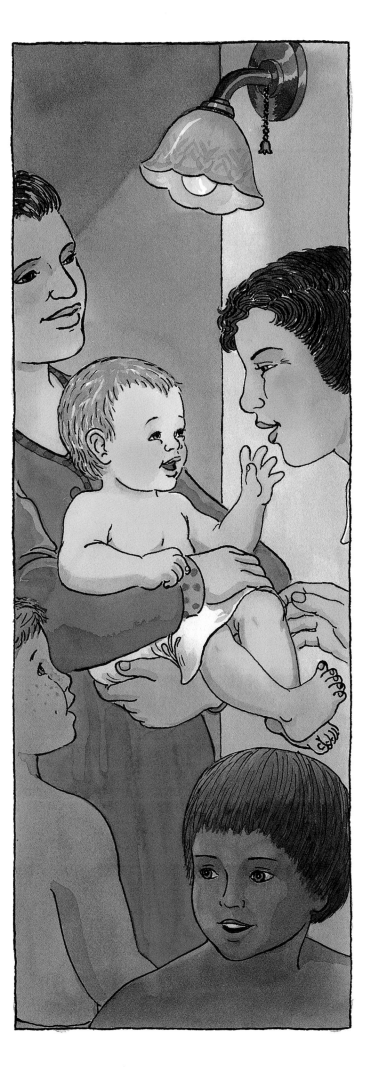

Ferryboats soon began taking passengers to Ellis Island, where papers were inspected and doctors made sure that people were healthy. This part was scary, because sick people could be sent back where they came from. Sometimes whole families were separated forever when healthy family members were allowed to stay in America and unhealthy ones had to leave.

When it was Ida, Sammy, and Ruthie's turn to be examined, a nurse complimented the children for being so clean. She kissed their heads and said that they were free to leave.

Almost as soon as they got onshore, the travelers took a long overnight train ride to Knoxville, Tennessee.

A large crowd was waiting at the railroad station to pick up passengers, and in the very front stood Yitta and her whole family.

Wearing his enormous grin, Abba made a high, dramatic leap from the train and kissed the ground. Soon everyone had gathered to watch as he made a big emotional speech, very eloquent, thanking God that he was in America, where he and his family could finally be free.

Abba and Pearl set out to become good citizens in their adopted country. They dressed in the American styles, learned to speak English, worked hard to earn a living for their family, and even had a fourth child, named Mariam, who was born on the Fourth of July. One Thanksgiving, Pearl brought Yitta a huge basket of fruit with money hidden in the bottom to offer thanks to Yitta and to repay her expenses for bringing everyone to America.

It has been almost eighty years since the Goodstein family arrived in America, and every year we still have an enormous Thanksgiving reunion of family members from across America and around the world, who tell one another all of the stories that have happened ever since.